RISE
TO THE
SKY

HOW THE WORLD'S
TALLEST TREES GROW UP

Rebecca E. Hirsch
illustrated by Mia Posada

M Millbrook Press / Minneapolis

In memory of my father, who taught me to love trees —R.E.H.

For H.J.L—my dad, one of the sturdiest trees I know —M.P.

Millbrook Press™
An imprint of Lerner Publishing Group, Inc.
241 First Avenue North
Minneapolis, MN 55401 USA

For reading levels and more information, look up this title at www.lernerbooks.com.

Additional back matter images: George Ostertag/Alamy Stock Photo (Douglas fir); petrenkoua/Getty Images (giant sequoia); Peter Unger/Getty Images (coast redwood); clkraus/Shutterstock (Sitka spruce); Florapix/Alamy Stock Photo (Kashmir cypress); Chien Lee/Minden Pictures (yellow meranti); Eucalyptus 99/Wikimedia Commons (Australian mountain ash); Bjorn Svennson/Science Photo Library (southern blue gum); Fourleaflover/Getty Images (map).

Designed by Kimberly Morales.
Main body text set in Handysans. Typeface provided by MADType.
The illustrations in this book were created using cut paper collage with watercolor.

Library of Congress Cataloging-in-Publication Data

Names: Hirsch, Rebecca E., author. | Posada, Mia, illustrator.
Title: Rise to the sky : how the world's tallest trees grow up / Rebecca E. Hirsch ; illustrated by Mia Posada.
Description: Minneapolis, MN, USA : Millbrook Press, [2023] | Includes bibliographical references. | Audience: Ages 5–10 | Audience: Grades 2–3 | Summary: "What are the tallest living things on Earth? Trees! Discover what growing trees need so they can rise to the sky in this lyrical look at the tree life cycle" —Provided by publisher.
Identifiers: LCCN 2022020384 (print) | LCCN 2022020385 (ebook) | ISBN 9781728440873 (lib. bdg.) | ISBN 9781728485669 (eb pdf)
Subjects: LCSH: Trees—Juvenile literature. | Trees—Life cycles—Juvenile literature.
Classification: LCC QK475.8 .H568 2023 (print) | LCC QK475.8 (ebook) | DDC 582.16—dc23/eng/20220608

LC record available at https://lccn.loc.gov/2022020384
LC ebook record available at https://lccn.loc.gov/2022020385

Manufactured in the United States of America
1-49857-49704-8/23/2022

What is the tallest living thing?

It's not an elephant

or a giraffe

or even a blue whale.

It's a tree!

Some trees rise more than three hundred feet into the sky. They can reach higher than the Statue of Liberty

SITKA
SPRUCE
(317 FEET)

STATUE
OF LIBERTY
(305.5 FEET)

AUSTRALIAN
MOUNTAIN ASH
(329.7 FEET)

GIRAFFE
(18 FEET)

YELLOW
MERANTI
(331 FEET)

KASHMIR
CYPRESS
(310 FEET)

AFRICAN
ELEPHANT
(13 FEET)

BLUE WHALE
(80 FEET)

or even the Big Ben clock tower.
How do they grow so tall?

BIG BEN
(316 FEET)

COAST
REDWOOD
(380.3 FEET)

SOUTHERN
BLUE GUM
(302 FEET)

GIANT
SEQUOIA
(314 FEET)

COAST
DOUGLAS FIR
(327 FEET)

The tallest trees spring from old stumps

or from seeds
as small as a ladybug

or a speck of dirt.

They sink their roots
into the earth and lift their leaves toward the light.

Growing trees are hungry.
They feed themselves with sunlight.
Their leaves use light from the sun,
water from the ground,
and carbon dioxide from the air
to make sugar and oxygen.

The sugar
becomes food
for the tree,

and the oxygen
becomes part
of the air we
breathe.

Growing trees are thirsty.

They drink deeply
through their roots.

They sip rain and fog
and last winter's snow.

Inside, the water climbs through tubes in the wood, rising all the way to the leaves.

Growing trees need air.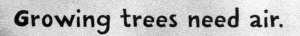

They breathe
through pinprick
holes in their leaves.

IN goes carbon dioxide!
OUT go oxygen and water!

The water becomes
clouds and fog,
and rain and snow,
and falls to the
ground
so the roots can
drink again.

On a steady diet of sunlight and water and air,
young trees grow up fast.

They rise . . .

UP to the sky!

Year after year,
they grow taller.

Year after year,
they grow wider,
with new wood
laid over old.

Their roots grow in an
ever-wider circle

and intertwine with the
roots of their neighbors.

Their roots become tough and hard
and help hold the tree up.

As centuries pass,
the tallest trees stand
in sunlight and fog,
in storms and fires.

Many have stood for thousands of years.

As the tallest trees tower
over the world,

they send down their seeds.

Inside each seed is a tiny
tree waiting to grow tall.

If the young trees can sink their roots and lift their leaves,

if they can get
plenty of air
and water and
sunlight . . .

someday
they too
might rise
to the sky.

Someday
they
might
become

the
tallest
trees.

How Does a Tall Tree Grow?

Trees have a body—an enormous body—made of different parts. The parts all work together.

LEAVES: Light energy from the sun is absorbed by chlorophyll, a pigment that gives leaves their green color. With the help of chlorophyll, leaves use the energy from sunlight to combine water and carbon dioxide into sugar and oxygen. This process is called photosynthesis. (*Photo* means "light," and *synthesis* means "joining together.")

STOMATA: These tiny holes in the leaves allow the tree to breathe. Carbon dioxide, oxygen, and water vapor flow through the holes.

ROOTS: Roots anchor a tree in the soil and help the tree stand. Tiny root hairs absorb water and minerals from the ground. A tall tree can drink hundreds of gallons each day. These trees do not tolerate dry spells. During a drought, the tree's leaves may droop, turn brown, or fall off. Eventually, without enough water, the tree may die.

BRANCH TIPS: Trees grow taller only at their tops and the tips of their branches. If a branch sprouts from the trunk a few feet off the ground, the branch will always remain that same distance from the ground, no matter how tall the tree grows.

XYLEM: These tubes in the wood carry water from the roots to the leaves. Leaves pull the water up through the tubes, just as you suck water upward through a straw.

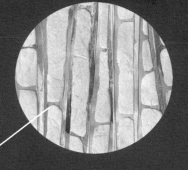

PHLOEM: The inner bark, called phloem, carries sugars from the leaves to the branches, trunk, and roots.

TRUNK: The trunk lifts the leaf-covered branches toward the sun. Every year, new wood is added under the bark. The wood forms rings, one ring for every year of the tree's age. You can count the rings in a cut stump to find out how old a tree is.

How Fast Can Tall Trees Grow?

The tallest trees can grow very fast, especially when they are young. An Australian mountain ash can grow 6.5 feet (2 m) per year! Unlike a person, trees grow taller only at their tops. If you were to grow this way, it would be like stacking a tower of hats on your head.

How Tall Can Trees Get?

Researchers think the tallest possible tree height may be 400 to 426 feet (122 to 130 m). As trees near their maximum height, they struggle to pull water up such a far distance. As the flow of water slows, the tree slows its growth. The top of the tree may die, even though the rest of the tree is still very much alive.

How Do You Measure a Tall Tree?

The most reliable way to measure the height of a tree is for someone to climb to the top. They use ropes to climb and take care not to damage the tree. Once they reach the top, they drop a tape measure to the ground. It is very dangerous work and should only be attempted by someone who has been trained to do it.

Were Trees Always This Tall?

A few hundred years ago, some trees may have been over 400 feet (122 m) tall. But people cut those giants down. Today the tallest tree, a coast redwood called Hyperion, stands 380.3 feet (115.9 m).

How Long Can Tall Trees Live?

The tallest trees can live a long time. Coast Douglas firs can live for more than one thousand years and coast redwoods for more than two thousand. But giant sequoias can live even longer. Some trees are over thirty-two hundred years old, which means there are giant sequoias alive today that sprouted when ancient Egypt was thriving.

Where Do the Tallest Trees Live?

You'll find the tallest trees in only a few parts of the world. They grow in mild climates with plenty of water and not much wind. The map shows the location of the tallest member of each tree species.

Sitka Spruce
Picea sitchensis
317 feet (96.6 m)
California, United States

Coast Douglas Fir
Pseudotsuga menziesii var. menziesii
327 feet (99.7 m)
Oregon, United States

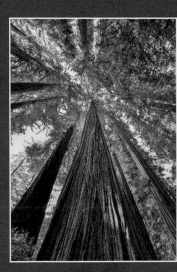

Coast Redwood
Sequoia sempervirens
380.3 feet (115.9 m)
California, United States

Giant Sequoia
Sequoiadendron giganteum
314 feet (95.7 m)
California, United States

Kashmir Cypress
Cupressus cashmeriana
310 feet (94.6 m)
Wangdue Phodrang, Bhutan

Yellow Meranti
Shorea faguetiana
331 feet (100.8 m)
Sabah, Borneo

Southern
Blue Gum
Eucalyptus globulus
302 feet (92 m)
Tasmania, Australia

Australian
Mountain Ash
Eucalyptus regnans
329.7 feet (100.5 m)
Tasmania, Australia

Activity: Up to the Top!

Explore how the leaves of trees suck up water. Collect leaves from a few different trees, snipping them with scissors at the base of the stem. Place the leaves in a drinking glass filled a third of the way with water. Add red or blue food coloring to the water. Observe the leaves closely over several days, using a magnifying lens if you have one. The color should gradually reach the leaves. The leaves are sucking the colored water up through xylem tubes in the stem.

Activity: How Tall?

Want to estimate the height of a tree without having to climb to the top with a tape measure? It's easy. All you need is a tape measure and a friend. Turn your back to the tree, spread your legs wide, bend forward, and look at the tree through your legs. If you can't see the top of the tree, move farther away and try again. When you can see the top of the tree through your legs, you are the same distance away as the height of the tree. With your friend's help, measure your distance from the tree with the tape measure. That's how tall the tree is!

Further Reading

Chin, Jason. *Redwoods*. New York: Roaring Brook, 2009.
This book explores the world of coast redwoods and takes you on a journey into the canopy.

Green, Jen, and Claire McElfatrick. *The Magic and Mystery of Trees*. New York: DK Publishing, 2019.
Discover more fascinating facts about how trees around the world live and grow.

Johnston, Tony, and Wendell Minor. *Sequoia*. New York: Roaring Brook, 2014.
Discover the majesty of a forest giant in this lyrical look at the life of a giant sequoia.

Judge, Lita. *The Wisdom of Trees: How Trees Work Together to Form a Natural Kingdom*. New York: Roaring Brook, 2021.
Learn how trees around the world communicate and cooperate, helping one another to survive.

Pearson, Carrie A., and Susan Swan. *Stretch to the Sun*. Watertown, MA: Charlesbridge, 2018.
Read about the tallest known tree, a coast redwood, and the community of plants and animals that live atop its branches.